MW01130288

YOGI BEAR'S
GUIDE TO PLANTS

by Mark Weakland
illustrated by Christian Cornia

Consultant:
Christopher T. Ruhland, PhD
Professor of Biological Sciences
Minnesota State University
Mankato, Minnesota

CAPSTONE PRESS
a capstone imprint

Visitors to Jellystone Park were arriving, but Yogi didn't see them. He was too busy looking at his garden.

"What are you doing, Yogi?" asked Boo Boo.

"Hey, hey, hey, it's a sunny day," said Yogi. "So I'm watching my garden grow. You can watch too, Boo Boo."

"I see lettuce, peppers, and carrots," said Boo Boo.

"I see a tasty salad," said Yogi, "to put in a pic-a-nic basket!"

"Everything is growing," said Boo Boo.

"It's the great outdoors at work," said Yogi. "Plants need soil, sunlight, and water to grow."

Soil contains
the nutrients
a plant needs
to grow.

"Most plants start as seeds," said Yogi. "Inside each seed is a living plant waiting to grow."

"What will those garden seeds become?" asked Boo Boo.

"Peas," explained Yogi. "And these will become sunflowers. Here, Boo Boo. Plant a future flower."

a plant growing
from a bean seed

Boo Boo looked up at a giant fir tree. "Boy, this tree is big!"

Yogi held up three fingers. "Big or small, most plants have the same parts—roots, stems, and leaves."

"Even trees?" asked Boo Boo.

"Sure," said Yogi. "Here are the roots. The needles are the leaves. And the trunk is the stem."

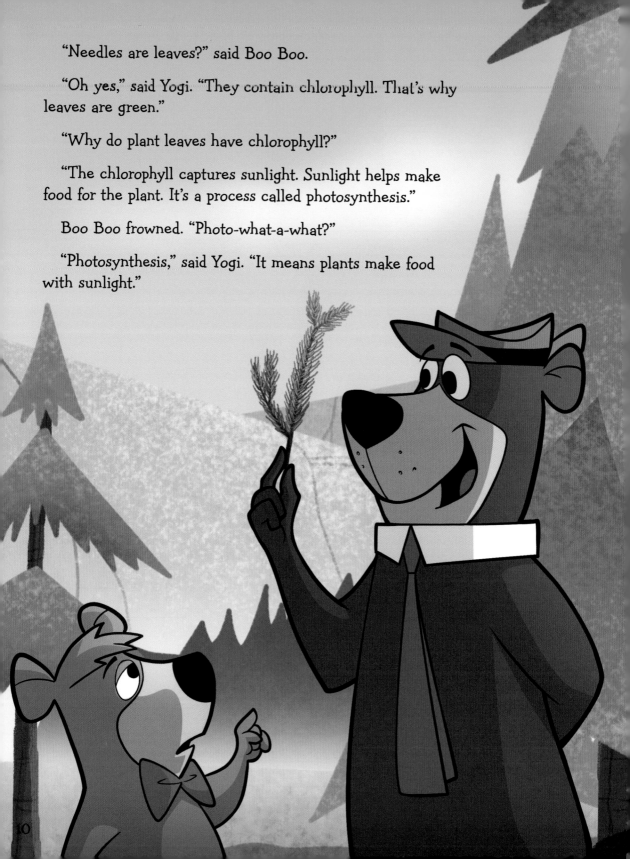

"Needles are leaves?" said Boo Boo.

"Oh yes," said Yogi. "They contain chlorophyll. That's why leaves are green."

"Why do plant leaves have chlorophyll?"

"The chlorophyll captures sunlight. Sunlight helps make food for the plant. It's a process called photosynthesis."

Boo Boo frowned. "Photo-what-a-what?"

"Photosynthesis," said Yogi. "It means plants make food with sunlight."

air

sunlight

Chlorophyll in plant leaves takes in sunlight.

A plant draws in water and nutrients through its roots and into its stem.

nutrients and water

During photosynthesis, plants absorb sunlight. They use sunlight, gas from the air, and water to make sugar. Plants use the sugar for food.

"If leaves make food, what do roots do?" asked Boo Boo.

"Roots take in water and nutrients from the soil," said Yogi. "They store food. Roots also support a plant and hold it in the ground."

"What about stems?" asked Boo Boo.

"Stems support the leaves," said Yogi. "And they carry nutrients and water to different parts of the plant."

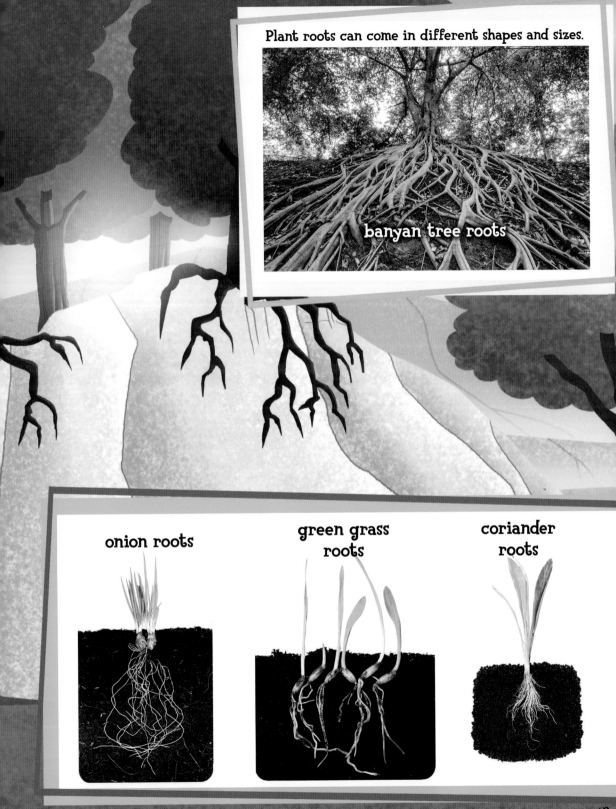

Plant roots can come in different shapes and sizes.

banyan tree roots

onion roots

green grass roots

coriander roots

13

"This plant is covered in flowers!" exclaimed Boo Boo.

"Many plants have flowers," said Yogi. "Flowers make seeds. And seeds make a new plant."

Yogi popped a berry in his mouth. "Lucky for us, many seeds are protected inside sweet fruits," said Yogi. "Have a berry, Boo Boo!"

Fruits can have different seeds.

A strawberry's seeds are on the fruit's skin.

An apple has seeds inside.

A peach has a large pit that covers the seed.

"To get to a good place to grow, seeds need to move around."
said Yogi.

"How do seeds move?" asked Boo Boo. "They don't have legs."

"Seeds can't walk, little buddy. But they can move in other
ways. The wind helps seeds fly through the air."

"Like a parachute!" exclaimed Boo Boo.

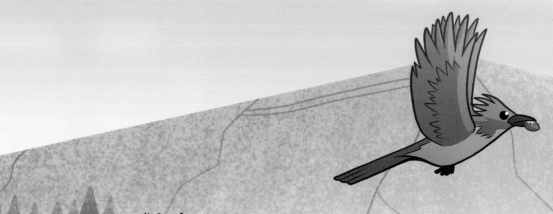

"You bet," said Yogi. "Seeds can also float in water, get
washed along by the rain, or ... "

"Or be carried away by animals like birds," said Boo Boo.

WAYS SEEDS MOVE

People plant seeds.

Wind blows dandelion seeds.

Coconut seeds float in water.

Animals like squirrels bury seeds.

Seeds get caught in an animal's fur.

"Yikes!" yelled Boo Boo.

Yogi grinned. "Hey, hey, hey, pinecones away!"

"Are falling pinecones another way to move seeds?" asked Boo Boo.

"Yes indeed, Boo Boo," said Yogi. "That pine tree is a conifer. That means the tree's seeds are in these pinecones. Redwood trees are also conifers."

Small seeds inside pinecones grow to be mighty pine trees.

seed

"Are oak and maple trees conifers?" asked Boo Boo.

"No," said Yogi. "Those trees are flowering plants."

"Flowering plants?" asked Boo Boo in surprise. "Like the berries we saw?"

"Yes," said Yogi. "These trees produce flowers, just like berry bushes, pumpkin vines, and tomato plants."

"Flowering plants make a lot of food," said Boo Boo. "Are those bees looking for food too?"

"Yes they are, little buddy," said Yogi. "The bees are collecting pollen and nectar to bring back to their hives. They also spread pollen to the other flowers they land on."

"That's no carpet you're lying on, Boo Boo," said Yogi. "It's moss."

"It's so soft," said Boo Boo.

"And different from your av-er-age plant," said Yogi. "Unlike most plants, moss has no stems, roots, or leaves. And it does not make flowers or seeds."

"No seeds?" asked Boo Boo. "How does new moss grow?"

"From tiny things called spores," said Yogi. "When a spore lands in a cool, moist place, new moss can begin to grow."

moss

"Look, Yogi," said Boo Boo. "Ferns!"

"Another type of plant," said Yogi. "Good eyes, Boo Boo."

"A fern is like moss in some ways, but different in others," said Yogi. "A fern makes spores, just like moss. Unlike moss, ferns can move water and nutrients in their stems."

ferns

"Boy, we've seen a lot of plants," said Boo Boo.

"Yes we have," said Yogi. "And every plant we've seen can be used by an animal. Caterpillars eat leaves, raccoons live in hollowed-out trees, birds gather grasses to build nests, bees collect pollen from flowers, and ..."

"And people use trees to make paper and build furniture!" exclaimed Boo Boo.

"Plants sure are important," said Boo Boo.

"You bet, little buddy," said Yogi. "In fact, there's another important reason we need plants."

"What's that, Yogi?" asked Boo Boo.

"For a tasty lunch!" exclaimed Yogi. "Plants produce the food we eat. Here, Boo Boo. Have a peanut butter and Jellystone sandwich!"

EXPLORE MORE!

Do you know why flowering plants produce fruit? Fruit holds and protects a plant's seeds. But a fruit's main purpose is to move a plant's seeds around.

Let's take a closer look at the different seeds inside fruits.

What You Need

+ an adult
+ a sharp knife
+ tools to remove the seeds, such as a small spoon, toothpick, or a pair of tweezers
+ paper towel

+ pencil and paper
+ small sandwich bags to put the seeds in
+ pieces of fruit: you can use fruits such as apples, lemons, strawberries, melons, kiwifruits, or tomatoes

What You Do

+ Ask an adult to cut open the fruit.
+ Use your spoon to dig through the fruit and find the seeds. Use a toothpick or tweezers to find small seeds.
+ Carefully remove the seeds from each fruit. Put the seeds on the paper towel.
+ Write down the number of seeds you find in each piece of fruit.
+ Put the seeds in small sandwich bags. Use a different bag for each fruit.
+ Compare the seeds in the bags. How are the seeds alike? How are they different?

Learn more about plants at **www.capstoneKids.com**.

Critical Thinking Using the Common Core

1. Most plants have the same three parts. What are they? (Key Ideas and Details)

2. Plant leaves contain chlorophyll. What is chlorophyll? (Craft and Structure)

3. What makes moss different from other plants? Use the text to help you with your answer. (Key Ideas and Details)

GLOSSARY

absorb—to soak up

chlorophyll—the green substance in plants that captures sunlight and helps plants make food

conifer—a plant that has needles and produces cones filled with seeds

fern—a plant with long, thin leaves and no flowers

hive—a place where bees live; thousands of bees live in one hive

moist—a little bit wet

moss—a soft, clumpy plant with green leaves and no flowers; moss usually grows in swamps and wetlands

nectar—a sweet liquid found in flowers; bees collect and eat nectar

nutrient—a substance a living thing needs to grow and stay healthy

parachute—a large piece of strong fabric; parachutes let people jump from high places and float safely to the ground

photosynthesis—the process by which plants make their food

pollen—tiny yellow grains made by flowers

process—a series of actions that create a result

root—the part of a plant that grows under the ground

soil—dirt or earth in which plants grow

spore—used by some plants to produce new plants

stem—the long main part of a plant from which the leaves and flowers grow

READ MORE

Rattini, Kristin Baird. *Seed to Plant*. National Geographic Readers. Washington, D.C.: National Geographic, 2014.

Rockwell, Lizzy. *Plants Feed Me.* New York: Holiday House, 2014.

Rustad, Martha E. H. *Plants in Spring.* All About Spring. North Mankato, Minn.: Capstone Press, 2013.

INTERNET SITES

FactHound offers a safe, fun way to find Internet sites related to this book. All of the sites on FactHound have been researched by our staff.

Here's all you do:

Visit *www.facthound.com*

Type in this code: 9781491465479

Super-cool stuff! Check out projects, games and lots more at **www.capstonekids.com**

INDEX

Published by Capstone Press,
1710 Roe Crest Drive, North Mankato, Minnesota 56003
www.capstonepub.com

Library of Congress Cataloging-in-Publication Data
Weakland, Mark, author.
Yogi Bear's guide to plants / by Mark Weakland.
pages cm. — (Yogi Bear's guide to the great outdoors)
Summary: "Popular cartoon character Yogi Bear introduces young readers to different types of plants at Jellystone, how they grow, and how they impact our environment"—Provided by publisher.
ISBN 978-1-4914-6547-9 (library binding)
ISBN 978-1-4914-6551-6 (eBook PDF)
1. Plants—Juvenile literature. I. Title. II. Title: Guide to plants. III. Series: Weakland, Mark. Yogi Bear's guide to the great outdoors.
QK49.Q23 2016
581—dc23
2014049171

Editorial Credits
Michelle Hasselius, editor; Ashlee Suker, designer;
Nathan Gassman, creative director; Tracy Cummins,
media researcher; Laura Manthe, production specialist

Image Credits
Shutterstock: Alex Staroseltsev, 15 Top, Bogdan Wankowicz, 7, Ethan Daniels, 17 Middle, infocus, 5, JanBussan, 17 Middle Left, mapichai, 11, Michael Warwick, 25, Noppanun K, 13 Top, nulinukas, 19 Left, Roman Samokhin, 15 Middle, Serg64, 19 Right, Sergey Peterman, 15 Bottom, Sergey Toronto, 23, showcake, 13 Bottom Left, 13 Bottom Right, Singkham, 17 Left, Sumikophoto, 17 Middle Right, Tom Reichner, 17 Right, Valentina Razumova, 13 Bottom Middle.

Printed in the United States of America in
North Mankato, Minnesota. 052015 008823CGF15

Books in this Series:

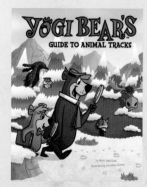

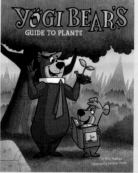